JANE WHALLEY PROST

Flavours
from the Flying
Gourmet

"Jane knows just how to feed the senses; her recipes look good, and taste even better. They are not too difficult to master, but they are surprising. Interesting ingredients, put together in appetising ways."

Janet Hull OBE

My sincere thanks to our photographer, Steve Campbell, not only for his obvious talent but for his wonderful sense of humour and generosity - a total joy to work with. See www.stevecampbell.tv

For Stéphane, my charming husband - without his encouragement, belief and support, this book would not have happened!

contents

INTRODUCTION

FOR THE LOVE OF COOKING

Ever since the day I threw my own 21st birthday party and people were amazed by the food I laid on, I have just kept on cooking.

On reflection, I suppose it was even before then that I got started. As a secretary, straight out of college and working as PA to the Managing Editor of the Telegraph Sunday Magazine, I had to be organised. Fortune had it that I could throw parties at my parents' house, often cooking for 50 people or so, plus house guests. My father let me have the budget if I did everything. I found cooking easy and people loved it.

A one-month advanced course at Leith's of London in my twenties taught me the principles of 'cordon bleu'. A ski season beckoned and, with the Leith's experience and references, a premier chalet in the Alps was on offer. Mégève, Courchevel and Méribel followed - I have been wintering in the Alps ever since, first as a chalet girl, then running my own catered chalet business, then as a freelance chef for high-end private chalet owners and now, as co-owner, with my husband, Stéphane, of a ski school and property management company, Méribel Connections.

In the early days summers were spent yachting, as front of house or chef on yachts in the Caribbean, the Côte d'Azur and the Great Barrier Reef; or in London - doing weddings, city lunches and cocktail parties for the sometimes rich and sometimes famous! Then, in 2001, Stef and I decided to find a property in the south west of France and La Cambe was born. After 10 years of renovation, between other things, the chef's kitchen was installed in 2011, and, in the summer of 2012, our cooking courses began.

So, what's my philosophy for delivering great food?

1. Fresh, good quality ingredients are key.

2. Certain things - like straining, reducing etc - are really worth taking time over to get the perfect intense flavour. It should explode in the mouth.

3. Texture is also very important - always to have contrast on the plate.

4. Sometimes simple is perfect. I look for short cuts as long as they don't jeopardise the flavour and taste.

5. Presentation is great fun. I aim to make food look as good as it tastes!

I've adored hosting residential and day courses over the last two years at La Cambe. We have had great clients, accompanied by partners and friends too, and they have made me feel very experienced and knowledgeable. It's because of them, the first people to place their confidence in me as a teacher, that I'm putting pen to paper now - they wanted the cookery book that went with the course and the experience, to remind them of all the good things they had learned and put into practice. I hope it works for you too.

Jane Whalley Prost

NOTE: Anyone can come to La Cambe, South West France, for a culinary experience – you don't have to take a cookery course! We offer bespoke holidays in beautifully luxurious and extremely spacious accommodation. Contact us to find out more at www.gourmetcookingholidays.com

CANAPES
& STARTERS

melon & parma ham shooter

Revisited as a canapé - deliciously refreshing

INGREDIENTS

- Canteloupe melon - fresh and ripe
- Prosciutto ham, thin slices, trimmed of fat
- Baking paper

METHOD

To dry the Parma ham, line a baking tray with baking paper. Lay out the slices of ham, not overlapping - normally 3 or 4 slices per tray (depending on the size of your baking tray). Then cover with a further sheet of baking paper, layer another 3 or 4 slices of ham and cover with another sheet of baking paper. Cover with another baking tray the same size so it keeps the ham flat.

Place in oven at 140°C for 50 minutes until it is crisp - remove and dab with paper towel and place on wire rack to cool.

Halve the melon. With a spoon scoop out the pips and discard. Cut each half into 4 and cut between skin and flesh. Chop into cubes. Then if you have a juicer, juice the melon. If you don't have a juicer, then pop the cubes into a liquidiser and purée until smooth. Pass through a strainer if necessary. Chill the liquid.

To serve, pour into shot glasses and top each glass with a piece of dried Parma ham. Alternate a nibble of ham then a sip of the melon juice... delicious!

Tip: One slice of prosciutto will do two people, but when drying the ham you might as well do at least 6 slices. With the rest you can serve as nibbles on their own, broken lengthwise and standing upright in a glass.

One melon will give you enough juice for 8-10 shooters.

blinis with smoked salmon or trout

A classic but worth it - you can make larger ones if you wanted to serve as a starter with some mixed salad leaves

For the blinis:
(you can make these in advance and they freeze well - makes 50-60)

- 1 egg
- 225ml milk
- 160g self-raising flour - if making for gluten free, just use a 50/50 mix of rice flour and buckwheat flour - slightly heavier but works well.
- 1 tbs dried dill
- Salt, pepper

For the topping:

- Smoked salmon or trout of good quality, 20g per person
- Lemon, cut into wedges and pips removed
- Crème fraîche
- Capers (optional)
- Fresh sprigs of dill, chives or coriander

METHOD

For the blinis: In a measuring jug, measure the milk, then add the egg and mix well with a fork. Add the flour and seasoning and make sure you have a batter with a ribbon-like consistency - either add a dash more milk or a little more flour. Let sit for 30 minutes.

Then heat a heavy-bottomed frying pan, brush with olive oil, then wipe with a piece of kitchen towel or use a pan spray - very little. Pour little rounds and wait for the air bubbles to show, then flip them over with a spatula. When cooked through and golden, remove and cool on wire rack.

For the topping: Slice the smoked fish into 2 cm x 3 cm strips and toss with fresh lemon juice, black pepper and chopped capers, if you like.

Warm the blinis briefly in the oven. Then place a small dollop of crème fraîche on each blini. Then fold over pieces of the smoked fish and place on top of the crème fraîche. Decorate with fresh sprigs of dill, chopped chives or coriander, as you wish, and serve.

Tip: You can freeze the remaining blinis for another time.

prawn soup
shooter or starter

Silky smooth and creamy - yet there's no cream or butter in the recipe

4

- 4 handfuls of cooked prawns, with heads and shells
- 1 onion, peeled and roughly chopped
- 1 carrot, washed and roughly chopped
- 1 bay leaf
- 3 black peppercorns
- White part of one leek, cleaned and roughly chopped
- 150ml white wine
- 1 tbsp tomato purée
- Lemon juice
- Chives

METHOD

Shell the prawns, keeping the shells and heads. Keep the prawns chilled.

Roast the shells and heads on a baking tray in the oven - 160°C for 15 minutes. Meanwhile, cook the onion, carrot and leek until soft - allow to brown slightly. Add the roasted heads and shells. Deglaze the pan with the wine. Add the peppercorns, bay leaf and water to cover. Allow to simmer for 25 minutes.

When cool, blend with hand blender until finely puréed. Pass through sieve and reserve the liquid - discard the rest. Add some tomato purée and a dash of lemon juice to flavour. Season with salt and pepper.

At this stage you can refrigerate the soup to use later. When serving as a shooter, heat the liquid through, then pour into shooter glasses and garnish with whole prawn and whole chive. (The rest of the prawns you can use in another recipe).

If serving as a soup, lightly heat the remaining prawns in olive oil or, if you feel like it, a small knob of butter. Season with salt and pepper. Put prawns at bottom of bowl and cover with soup. Garnish with chopped chives and a dollop of crème fraîche.

Serves 4 as a soup or 8-10 shooters.

Tip: If you reduce to the consistency of a thick sauce, it can be used as a sauce for any white fish.

watermelon spoons or salad

A great summer canapé or salad – a refreshing and beautiful combination

INGREDIENTS

- 1/4 seedless watermelon, cut into small diced pieces
- 1 tbs dehydrated chopped black olives or just stone and chop some black olives - see glossary for drying black olives
- 1 tbs pumpkin seeds
- 125g feta cheese - cut into small cubes, same size as watermelon

METHOD

Mix the watermelon, pumpkin seeds and feta together - gently. Add the black olives just before serving, otherwise they will bleed and look unattractive.

As a canapé, served on spoons, they are colourful and full of fresh summer flavour.

As a salad, cut the melon and feta into bigger pieces - a fresh and exciting touch.

Serves 6 as a salad or 12 canapés.

crème de foie gras brûlée

The way to a man's heart!

This can be used as a 'mise en bouche' or pre-starter or if you are serving canapés and nibbles and your guests are able to use two hands. I often do this for casual entertaining - serve a variety of canapés, dips or such and then sit down at the table direct to the main course.

INGREDIENTS

- 135g foie gras mi-cuit - best to make it yourself, see recipe p 16. If not possible, always buy farm-made French foie gras since they are kind to their ducks.
- 250g double cream
- 3 egg yolks
- Salt and pepper
- Icing sugar for dusting

METHOD

Mix all ingredients, except the sugar, with a stick blender until smooth. Strain and pour into little ramekins. Place ramekins in a bain marie (water bath) in oven at 85°C for 25 minutes.

Remove from oven and allow to cool. Cover and refrigerate at least four hours. Then remove from fridge and dust with icing sugar. Then using a blowtorch, heat the tops until they form a crispy crust.

Makes 8-10 little ramekins.

crispy triangles filled with goat's cheese & sundried tomatoes or leek & brie

Great for canapés or on a salad for a light lunch

For goat's cheese filling (makes 20):

- 5 rectangular brick sheets - available in most supermarkets but you can substitute filo pastry.
- 100g goat's cheese
- 4 sun-dried tomatoes - chopped finely
- 1 tbsp fig jam
- Fresh basil - chopped

METHOD

Mix the filling ingredients together with a fork. Then cut each brick layer into four strips approximately 6 cm wide. If using filo, you need to have a damp tea towel to cover the rest while you work with the sheets - best to use two sheets and brush each with melted butter to make them hold together.

Place a teaspoon of mixture on the end of the strip, then take one corner and fold across on the diagonal to form a triangular shape, then fold forward, then diagonally and continue folding until you have reached the end of the strip and have a neat tight triangle. Use melted butter or oil to seal the parcels.

Place on lined baking tray and pop into fridge for at least one hour prior to cooking at 160°C for 10 to 15 minutes.

INGREDIENTS

For leek and Brie filling (makes 20):

- 1 leek, washed and finely-chopped
- 100g Brie, chopped
- 1 tsp whole cumin
- 5 brick leaves or 10 filo sheets, as above

METHOD

Wash the leek thoroughly and chop finely. Sauté the leek in some olive oil and butter until it is soft, about 20 minutes. Do not let it burn.

Mix the ingredients, not the brick leaves, together and season with salt and pepper.

Cut each brick layer into four strips, approximately 6 cm wide. Place a teaspoon of mixture on the end of the strip, then take one corner and fold across on the diagonal to form a triangular shape, then continue folding until you have reached the end of the strip and have a neat tight triangle. Use melted butter or oil to seal the parcels.

Place on baking tray, on baking paper and pop into fridge for at least one hour before cooking at 160°C for 10 to 15 minutes.

sushi maki rolls

Much easier than they look

- 100g fresh fish - wild salmon, tuna or prawn
- 1 avocado
- 1/2 cucumbor pceled, seeded
- 1/2 lemon, cut into wedges
- Sushi rice, 250g
- Water, 330ml
- Rice wine vinegar, 3 tbs
- Sugar, 1 tbs
- Salt
- 6 Nori seaweed sheets
- Wasabi
- Ginger slivers - marinated
- Soy sauce

METHOD

Rinse the rice, then cover with twice as much water. Bring to boil, cover. Lower heat. Cook for a further 10-15 minutes until water absorbed. Leave covered for further 15 minutes.

Meanwhile, heat the wine vinegar (apple cider if you don't have rice wine vinegar) with the salt and sugar till the sugar and salt have dissolved.

Spread rice out in a large flat dish, then drizzle the vinegar mix over and gently fold in. Then cover with a damp cloth and allow rice to cool to room temperature.

Prepare the fish - cut into 1/2 cm thick batons. Ensure no bones or skin. Cut the avocado in half and remove seed and skin. Cut the avocado into 1/2 cm thick batons and set aside in a bowl with lemon juice squeezed over. Cut the cucumber into 1/2 cm thick batons.

Place a nori seaweed sheet, smooth side down, on a sushi mat and spread out rice in a thin layer, leaving a 4 cm band at the far end with no rice. Half way up the rice, make a little indentation laterally. With tip of knife put a tiny amount of wasabi in the indentation - all the way across. Then place batons of fish or prawn and avocado or cucumber on top, making a line of filling lengthwise across the middle of the rice. Then with the help of the mat, roll it away from you, keeping the roll tightly packed. Dip your fingers in some water and dab across the 4 cm band at the end and seal the roll. Then wrap in cling film and refrigerate until ready to cut and serve. Have a tall measuring cup of hot water ready on your worktop. Cut the ends off each roll so you have clean neat ends. Dip the knife into the water and dry with a paper towel between each cut. Cut each roll into 5 or 6 pieces.

Serve with bowls of soy sauce, some wasabi and a pile of the marinated slivered ginger. Eat with chop sticks.

Makes about 30 rolls, depending on how large you want them.

roasted aubergine
& herb toasts

The smoky flavour of the aubergine... mmmmm!

- 1 glossy aubergine
- 1 small onion, finely chopped
- 1 garlic clovo, minced
- Handful of mixed herbs
- 1 tbs lemon juice
- 1 tbs olive oil
- Salt and pepper
- 40g cream cheese or 1 tbs tahini paste

METHOD

Cut the aubergine in half lengthwise. Cut a diagonal pattern in its flesh. Brush with olive oil and season well. Place on baking sheet and roast in the oven at 170°C for 35-45 minutes depending on the size of the aubergine - the flesh should feel very soft.

Remove from oven and allow to cool. Sauté the onion and garlic in some olive oil until soft and lightly browned. Scoop out the flesh of the aubergine and mix with all the other ingredients, blending with a handheld blender or a little liquidiser until it is smooth. Taste and adjust the seasoning. You can add ground cumin, cayenne or paprika.

Spread over little toasts (using day-old French baguettes - wrap in tea towel overnight so they are soft). Slice thinly, place on an oven tray and drizzle olive oil, seasoning with salt and pepper and herbes de Provence if you like. Cook for 25 minutes at 130°C. Allow to cool and store in an airtight container.

Use as required. Garnish with snipped chives or other herbs.

Makes enough for 20-25 toasts.

salmon ceviche

Wonderful flavour combinations

- 300g fresh salmon
- 1 tbs finely-chopped shallot
- 1 tbs finely-chopped ginger
- 1 pink grapefruit - segmented, then chop the flesh but keep the juice
- Juice of 1 lime
- 1 red chilli, seeded and finely-chopped
- Soy sauce - 5 drops
- 1 tbs chopped capers
- 2 tbs goji berries
- 1 tsp honey
- 1 tsp fish sauce
- Fresh coriander and dill, chopped - keep some whole leaves for garnish

METHOD

Skin, bone and chop the salmon into small cubes.

Mix all ingredients together and leave to marinate for at least 2 hours.

Put into small glasses and serve with toasted pumpernickel or good granary bread.

Serves 6 as a starter or served in canapé spoons, makes 15-20.

grilled asparagus spears

A sure sign summer is on its way!

INGREDIENTS

- Fresh asparagus spears,
  about 6 per person
- Pine nuts
- Parma ham slices, cut into small pieces
- Dried black olives (see glossary)
- Fresh Parmesan
- Olive oil dressing
  (see vinaigrette dressing, p 45)

METHOD

Trim the spears - break off where the stem starts to harden or just cut with a knife. Blanch the asparagus for 2 minutes. Refresh in ice cold water for 1 minute, to stop the cooking, then drain. Dry off and place on hot griddle pan to make light burn marks.

Sauté the chopped ham and pine nuts with some olive oil, until ham is crispy and nuts are golden.

For the dressing - mix mustard, vinegar or lemon juice, olive oil, salt and pepper.

Toss the grilled spears through the dressing. Plate the asparagus and spoon the ham mix over the spears. Garnish with dried olives and shavings of parmesan. Add freshly-ground black pepper.

foie gras mi-cuit

(Seasoned, compressed and lightly cooked pure duck liver)

Delightful - it is NOT a pâté!!

For the mi-cuit:

- 1 whole fresh duck liver (not more than 500g)
- Salt, pepper
- Spices - marjoram, mace, ground clove, cardamom, a pinch of each
- 1 tsp brown sugar
- 1 tbs Armagnac

To serve:

- Fig or onion chutney, preferably homemade
- Toasted bread - not white, but not too strong in flavour - granary
- Herb and mesclun salad dressed with light vinaigrette of walnut oil and walnut vinegar, dash of mustard, salt and pepper.

To drink:

- Serve a chilled sweet white wine, such as Monbazillac or certain vins vendange tardive (late harvested), Sauternes or Jurançon

Take the whole duck liver (at room temperature), separate the two lobes and de-vein the liver gently. Place a sheet of clingfilm on your work surface, place the de-veined liver on that and season with salt and pepper, the spices and sugar and then splash some Armagnac over. Continue to add liver until you have a square of liver approximately 15 cm x 15 cm and 2 cm high. From one liver you have sufficient to make two "rolls" of foie gras mi-cuit.

Roll it up in the clingfilm and tighten so that the liver is very tightly compressed with no air gaps at all. Tie the ends. Then wrap with muslin to ensure it is really tightly rolled, but with minimal handling. Tie the ends. Bring a saucepan of boiling water to the boil, adding a glass of white wine, if you like. Then place the rolls in one at a time, for 1 minute 30 seconds. Remove and allow to cool before putting in fridge. When thoroughly chilled, if you have a vacuum packer, use it!

It is ready after two days, and will keep for up to a week.

To serve, cut with a wire cutter or very sharp knife dipped into a cup of boiling water between each cut. Slice into rounds and sprinkle with sea salt. Serve with warm toasts, a spoon of chutney and a fresh mesclun or herb salad.

Each roll will serve 6-8 as a starter.

spring rolls

Delicious flavours

- Rice wrappers, 2 or 3 per person, depending on appetite
- 200g minced cooked meat - pork, chicken or turkey
- 1 red chilli, seeded and minced
- Coriander, 1 tbs chopped
- Beansprouts, 2 handfuls
- 1 onion, chopped finely
- 1/2 red pepper, finely julienned
- 1 cm ginger, peeled and minced
- 1 carrot, peeled and finely julienned
- Sesame seed oil

METHOD

Sauté the onion, red pepper, carrot and ginger in the sesame seed oil until soft, then add the beansprouts and cook until softened. Place in a bowl with the other ingredients and mix well.

Soak the wrappers one by one in a shallow dish of cold water. Takes about 30-50 seconds to soften - needs to be pliable but not to have absorbed too much water. You will get the hang of it and become a production line, popping one wrapper into the water as you start rolling the previous one, but start one by one! Take out and place on a clean tea towel, absorbing excess water with a second tea towel or folding over the first. The wrapper must be dry.

Place a tablespoon of the mixture on the wrapper (on the tea towel) closest to you, form into an oblong shape with your fingers, then roll, keeping the mixture in tight, then fold in either side and continue to roll. Place on a tray lined with baking paper. Continue until all the mixture is used or you have enough.

Either use as they are or cook in a deep fat fryer till golden.

Serve with a dipping sauce and a little julienned carrot and roquette salad on the side.

DIPPING SAUCE FOR SPRING ROLLS: INGREDIENTS

- 1 shallot - minced
- 1 carrot - finely diced
- 1 red chilli - deseeded and finely chopped
- 1 tsp ginger, minced
- 1 tbs brown sugar
- 150g rice vinegar
- Fish sauce - a good splash
- Soy sauce or tamari - little splash
- 1 tbs olive oil
- 1 tbs fresh coriander - finely chopped

Heat the rice vinegar with the sugar until the sugar is dissolved. Cool and add other ingredients.

Serve in small bowls on a platter with the spring rolls. This makes enough filling for about 20 rolls.

pan-fried scallops

On a bed of buttery leeks with a balsamic reduction

- One leek, washed, trimmed and cut finely on the diagonal
- 4 large scallops, without coral
- Butter and olive oil
- Balsamic reduction (see glossary)
- Chopped dried seaweed to go round the edge (optional)

METHOD

Soften the chopped leeks in the butter with a dash of oil to stop it burning, over low heat until they are tender, about 20 minutes. Then you can allow them to brown ever so slightly. Keep warm.

Meanwhile, trim the scallops, ensuring that you check each one for the tough piece attached to the side. Sometimes it has already been removed in the shucking process. If not, then it will pull off, leaving the soft, perfect scallop in one piece. Dry and then make diagonal incisions across either the top or the bottom, not both. Then when all is ready to assemble, heat some oil in a non-stick pan. When nicely hot, place the scallops cut side down in the pan and cook until they are golden on one side. Flip over and then turn the heat down very low. Add a knob of butter and using a teaspoon, spoon the butter over the scallops.

Remove from heat. Place the leeks on the plate then put a scallop on top - sprinkle with sea salt and drizzle some balsamic reduction at the side.

If your scallops have coral, then separate before cooking. You can brown the tough muscle of the scallop with the corals in a dash of olive oil. Remove and discard. Deglaze pan with some white wine. Thoroughly scrape off all the brown bits. Add a knob of butter. Strain, cool, then store in an airtight jar and use over any fresh white fillet of fish.

Serves 4 as a starter.

hot duck's liver (escalope de foie gras chaud) served on a corn pancake

Heavenly - always use farm-fresh foie gras

- 200g/one lobe fresh duck liver, cut on the diagonal into 2.5 cm wide slices
- Salt
- Sweetcorn - 75g
- 3 eggs
- 80g flour
- 100g milk
- Balsamic vinegar
- Honey
- Butter

METHOD

For the pancake (it's a thick pancake!):

Mix eggs, flour and milk to form a batter and add the corn. Season with salt and pepper. Let sit for at least 30 minutes.

Oil some 5 cm circles 2 cm high. Then melt some butter in a pan and pour the batter into the circles. Using a blowtorch, seal the top and after a couple of minutes flip over. Cook until firm. Extract from the circles using spatula and tongs, if they don't slide out. Keep warm in the oven on low heat (140°C). Or this can be done in advance and reheated.

At this stage you must be ready to serve the liver and sauce.

For the liver:

Score the surface of one side of the liver in a diagonal pattern with a sharp knife.

Heat a dry pan and sear the liver on the scored side until it is golden, approximately one minute. Then reduce heat and sear other side. Then transfer to paper towel on a baking tray and place in warm oven (140°C) for 6-8 minutes while you make the sauce.

For the sauce:

Using the same pan, drain off any excess fat. Then deglaze the pan with some balsamic vinegar and honey (1 tbs per person of each) and reduce. When it gets syrupy, add 1 tbs of water to get to the right consistency. Then add a small knob of butter. Season with salt and check the balance. Adjust accordingly – if too sweet, add some more balsamic, if too acidic, add some more honey.

Then place the warm pancake on to warm plates - shallow bowls are good for this. Set on top the slice of liver and pour the sauce round the outside. Season the liver with some salt and serve.

Tip: A duck liver should be between 400g/450g.

Serves 4.

carpaccio of scallops

Fresh and light

- 8 large fresh scallops without coral
- Rice wine vinegar, 1 tbs
- Juice of 1 lemon
- Juice of 1 lime
- 1 tsp agave syrup
- Tomato - peeled, seeded and chopped into fine, small dice
- Pink peppercorns
- Sprigs of dill for garnish
- Salt

This is a cross between carpaccio, which is thinly sliced and raw, and ceviche, which is marinated, so the scallop is 'cooked' by the acid in the marinade.

METHOD

Mix the vinegar, lemon and lime juice with the peppercorns and agave. Clean the scallops and remove the coral, if there, and use for sauce in another recipe. Be sure to take off the hard lump of attached muscle - if you run your fingers around the edge of the scallop you will feel the change in texture and it will peel off very simply. Discard. Thinly slice the scallops, add to the marinade and place in fridge for one hour.

Arrange the slices in a flat bowl and pour over some of the dressing, then sprinkle with some tomato dice and sprigs of dill. Season with salt and serve with whole wheat, rye or pumpernickel toasts.

roasted red pepper, goat's cheese & aubergine starter

Delicious, elegant and easy to prepare ahead of time for a dinner party

- 4 roasted and peeled red peppers
- 120g goat's cheese
- Aubergine - sliced in thin rounds, approx 0.3 cm thick
- Fresh basil
- Olive oil

METHOD

To roast the peppers, place them under a grill until the skin is blackened and blistered - you have to keep turning them. Then place in a bowl and cover with cling film until cool. The skin will just peel off and you can remove the seeds from the inside and cut out the stalk. Open out down one side and spread them out on a chopping board. Cut out rounds the size of a ramekin - you need three layers. You should be able to get three rounds out of each pepper.

Pan-fry the aubergine slices in olive oil until browned lightly. Remove as they are done and drain on paper towel.

Prepare the ramekins and lightly oil them. Then layer them starting with the red pepper skin side down (without skin, but the shiny smooth side down - since, when you "turn them out" this will be the top).

Spread or slice the goat's cheese giving a thin layer, then add the aubergine - maybe two or three rounds depending on the size of the aubergine and the ramekin. Continue alternating red pepper, cheese and aubergine until the ramekin is full. Press down well and wrap with cling film, then stack in the fridge until ready to use.

Put aside four sprigs of basil for garnish, then finely mince the rest of the basil mixed with olive oil, using a hand-held mixer. Season with salt and pepper and add 1 tsp of icing sugar if needed.

Microwave the ramekins until hot – how long it takes depends on how powerful your microwave is. Allow them to sit until they stop bubbling. Then turn out onto individual plates, drizzle basil dressing round and garnish each with a sprig of fresh basil. Serve with a rye toast lightly spread with some tapenade on it (for homemade tapenade see p 101).

Serves 4.

SALADS, VEGETABLE DISHES & SAUCES

These dishes can be used as starters or lunch dishes

fig, roquette & gorgonzola salad

When fresh figs are available, this makes a great lunch dish!

INGREDIENTS

- Fresh figs - 2 per person
- Gorgonzola - 50g per person
- Slices of Parma ham, 2 per person
- Roquette - a handful each
- Salad vinaigrette (see p 45)
- 1 tbs dried black olives (see glossary)

METHOD

Toss the roquette leaves with the salad dressing, then place in the centre of either one big platter or individual plates. Loosely roll each piece of ham, place on salad. Then cut open one of the figs, so that you can place it in the centre of the ham slices, and put a dollop of the creamy ripe Gorgonzola on top. Quarter the other fig and place decoratively on the plate. Sprinkle some dried black olives to add to the salty contrast with the sweetness of the figs, the creaminess of the Gorgonzola and saltiness of the ham.

If serving on one large oblong platter, loosely wrap a slice of Parma ham round the base of an opened fig and pop a dollop of the cheese in the middle, then continue like that down the centre of the plate.

quinoa salad

A delicious and healthy option

INGREDIENTS

- 100g each of red and white quinoa
- Spring onions - finely chopped on the bias
- Parsley, mint and coriander - a good handful of each, chopped
- 1/2 Preserved lemon - finely diced
- Juice of 1 lemon
- Olive oil
- Salt and pepper
- Sunflower and pumpkin seeds, 1 tbs each
- 2 tbps goji berries

METHOD

Cook the red and white quinoa together. Drain and allow to cool. Chop scallions, herbs, tomatoes and mix in with a mix of seeds - pumpkin and sunflower. Add the goji berries.

You can make a little dressing of a teaspoon of mustard, olive oil with lemon juice, black pepper and salt. Mix through and let sit for 30 minutes before serving, so the goji berries can rehydrate from the moisture in the dish. It is not necessary to soak them first.

Serves 4.

fennel & pomegranate salad

The nutty anise flavour of fennel combines beautifully with the tart sweetness of the pomegranate fruit - good for digestion and your heart!

INGREDIENTS

- Fennel 1 bulb, cut into thin slices - easiest with a mandoline
- Pomegranate seeds, detached and separated
- Feta 80g - cut into small pieces
- 2 tbs olive oil
- Tarragon leaves, chopped
- Parsley - chopped 2 tbs
- Preserved lemon, 1/4, chopped
- Whole cumin - 1 tsp
- Piment d'espelette, 1/2 tsp

METHOD

Make the dressing by mixing olive oil and the ingredients listed, then mix the slivers of fennel and the pomegranate seeds with the dressing. Then add the feta.

Depending on the ripeness of the pomegranate, cut it in half and then tap with a wooden spoon and the seeds will just tumble out. If they don't, you have to gently assist their removal from the membrane with your fingers.

grilled mediterranean vegetable salad

Can be served warm or cold

INGREDIENTS

- 2 courgettes, cut into thin slices, lengthwise - if you have a mandoline it is quicker
- 2 red peppers, roasted, peeled and deseeded
- 1 aubergine, cut into 0.5 cm thick rounds
- Handful of fresh basil
- Olive oil
- Rock salt

METHOD

You will need a ridged cast-iron pan for this. Prepare all the vegetables and a serving dish. Heat the pan, then in batches place the courgette slices and aubergine rounds until they are scored by the ridges on the pan. Do not burn!

When each strip or round is cooked, remove from heat and place in serving dish and brush with olive oil, generous black pepper and salt.

Reheat if necessary, but this dish is great served warm or cold as a side dish. Chop the basil just before serving and toss through, with some more olive oil and lemon juice to taste.

roquette, orange & pink grapefruit salad

Great with barbecued chicken dishes or marinated roasted chicken legs

- 2 oranges
- 2 pink grapefruit
- 2 handfuls of roquette
- 1 handful of mint leaves
- 1 handful of coriander leaves
- 2 tbs toasted pine nuts
- Olive oil, salt and pepper
- 1 tbsp honey or agave syrup

Segment the oranges and grapefruits, squeezing out the juice at the end to make a dressing. You can reduce the juices down to 2 tbsp to intensify the flavour. Chop the mint and coriander leaves. Mix the reduced juice with the olive oil, honey, salt and pepper. Toss all together just before serving.

sweet potato & goat's cheese tart, with a gluten-free crust

Also makes a great tasty lunch, served with a mixed leaf salad

INGREDIENTS

If you want regular pastry, use the sweet dough (p 103), leaving out the sugar, vanilla and ground almonds. (quantities for a 30 cm diameter tart tin)

- Rice flour 40g
- Corn meal finely ground, 40g
- Buckwheat flour, 40g
- 45g butter - broken into pieces
- 60g Parmesan - grated
- 1 egg
- 1 tsp caraway seeds
- Salt and pepper

For the filling:

- Onion - coarsely chopped
- 2 sweet potatoes, peeled and cut into small cubes
- Large handful of fresh spinach leaves, stalks removed
- Goat's cheese 60g
- 2 eggs, beaten, and some milk

METHOD

Make the pastry first, put the flours in the bowl of a food processor and mix. Add the pieces of butter and the grated cheese, caraway seeds, salt and pepper. Mix on pulse mode until butter is all broken up, like breadcrumbs. Add the egg to the bowl and pulse until the mixture forms a ball or is nearly starting to stick together. If necessary, add 1 tbs of cold water.

Turn out onto floured baking paper and roll out to fit a tart tin 30 cm x 10 cm if rectangular, or 20-25 cm diameter if round. Then place in fridge to rest.

Sauté the onions in some olive oil with some garlic if you like and the sweet potato until the onions are soft and the sweet potato has some colour. Add the spinach and toss through. Then arrange the sweet potato mix in the tart base and dot with the goat's cheese. Then add egg milk mix (beaten lightly together with a fork and seasoned).

Pre-heat oven to 170°C - Pop in oven on metal oven tray for 40-45 minutes.

Serves 8.

black rice with vegetables

Another healthy option, gluten free, as is quinoa, and full of antioxidants
(used in pan fried sea bream dish, p 54)

INGREDIENTS	METHOD

INGREDIENTS

- Black rice - a handful per person and one for the pot
- 1 onion, finely diced
- 2 courgettes, diced
- Garlic - crushed to a paste
- Olive oil
- Goji berries, 1 tbs
- Handful of pumpkin and or sunflower seeds, optional
- Fresh chopped herbs, whatever you have to hand

METHOD

Sauté the onions in some olive oil until soft, add the garlic and courgettes - mix well and then up the heat a bit and let them brown a little.

Cook the rice according to instructions. Drain and rinse well. Season. Mix with vegetables and goji berries. Reheat in pan when ready to to serve. Stir through chopped herbs.

butternut squash, roasted

A beautiful vegetable dish to go with meat and fish dishes or stand alone

INGREDIENTS

- 1 butternut squash, peeled and seeds removed
- 1 red onion, chopped into small strips
- Garlic cloves in their skins
- 1 tsp whole cumin
- Olive oil, salt and pepper

METHOD

Pre-heat oven to 170°C. Cut the squash into cubes and place on a non-stick baking sheet or line a baking sheet with a Tefal sheet. Season with the cumin, salt and pepper and drizzle olive oil over. Mix well to make sure the squash is well coated. Roast for 20 minutes. Meanwhile sauté the onion with some olive oil and season. Add to the squash with the garlic and roast a further 20 minutes until all is soft and golden.

Serves 6.

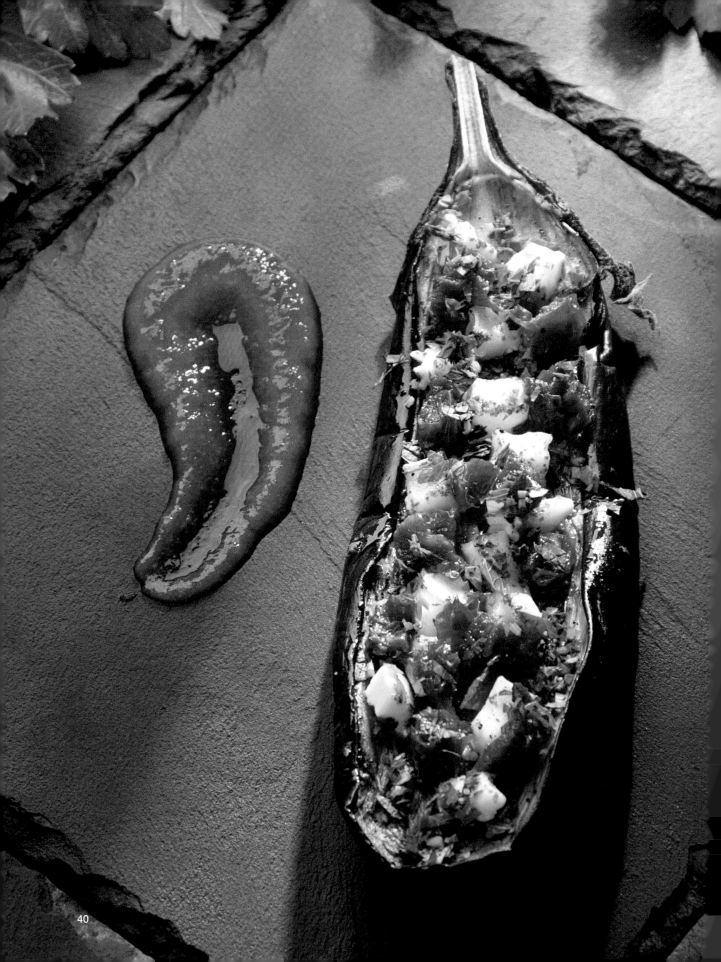

roasted stuffed aubergines

A starter, or a vegetarian main course

- 2 glossy aubergines - choose small ones for a starter or larger ones for a main
- 2 tomatoes - peeled and seeded, then chopped
- 1 chopped onion or 2 chopped shallots, sautéed in olive oil
- 1 clove crushed garlic - roast unpeeled for 10-15 minutes with the aubergine for sweeter flavour

- 2-4 sun-dried tomatoes, chopped
- Basil or parsley, to taste - finely chopped
- Goat's cheese, use a creamy one
- Olive oil
- Salt and pepper

Cut the aubergines in half lengthwise. Score the flesh. Rub the olive oil, salt and pepper into the flesh, then place skin side down on a baking sheet. Place in 170°C oven and cook for 30 to 50 minutes, depending on size, until the centre is soft. Remove and leave to cool.

Then spoon out the soft interior and mash thoroughly, adding some olive oil. Mix with rest of ingredients, removing the skin from the cooked garlic, and then refill the aubergine skins and dot the top with extra goat's cheese and the sun-dried tomatoes and return to oven until warm. Sprinkle with fresh herbs before serving.

Serve with delicious rich tomato sauce, see p 47.

Serves 4.

ratatouille

Wonderful vegetable dish, rich in colour and flavour - can be used on its own as a starter

- 1 onion, peeled and diced
- 1 garlic clove, crushed to a paste
- 1 red pepper, deseeded and diced
- 1 aubergine, diced
- 1 courgette, diced

- 1 glass white wine
- 400g tinned tomatoes, peeled and crushed. If you want to be a purist you can use fresh, but you must peel and seed them first!
- Lots of fresh thyme

METHOD

Sauté the onions, add the garlic, then the red pepper, the aubergine, and finally the courgettes. You don't want to overcook it - you want the vegetables to just 'catch'. Add some white wine, reduce, then lower heat and add the tomatoes. Black pepper, salt and lots of fresh thyme. Allow to simmer for at least 15 minutes.

Great served using a mould to form a cylindrical shape, then stick a sprig of thyme in the top. Put the thyme into the ratatouille before you have removed the mould, pressing down around the sprig so it all holds firm while you serve.

Serves 6.

sauce vierge

Great sauce for grilled white fish

INGREDIENTS

- 1 tsp coriander seeds - heated and then ground in pestle
- 1 clove garlic, crushed to a fine paste
- Salt
- Olive oil
- 1 tomato, peeled, seeded and diced
- Juice of one lemon
- 1 tbs each of tarragon, basil and coriander, chopped at last minute

METHOD

Mix all ingredients except the herbs, which should be added just before serving. Alternatively you can purée the herbs with all the ingredients, except the tomatoes. Then swirl the sauce round your fish and dot with the diced tomatoes.

Good with grilled fish and chicken dishes.

salsa verde

Delicious with barbecued meat or fish

INGREDIENTS

- 2 handfuls of fresh herbs - parsley, basil, tarragon - whatever you have in your garden
- 1 garlic clove
- 1 tbs capers - rinsed and drained
- Anchovies, according to taste
- Olive oil
- Lemon juice
- 1 tsp Dijon mustard
- 1 tbs red wine vinegar

METHOD

Blend everything together until you have a lovely rich green sauce - very much according to taste.

great salad vinaigrette

Good with all salads and steamed asparagus (green beans too)

INGREDIENTS

- 1 tsp Dijon mustard
- 2 tbs vinegar of your choice or lemon juice
- 4 tbs good quality olive oil
- Salt and pepper to taste

METHOD

Either put in a glass jar, put the lid on and shake vigorously or mix with fork in the salad dish - add the salad leaves and other ingredients for your salad and then when you serve, just mix through.

You can replace the vinegar with reduced fruit juice. 1/2 litre of apple juice reduced down to 2 tbs gives a great, intense flavour - try with other juices.

thai sauce

Great with all grilled meats and fish

- 1 tsp minced ginger
- 1 small shallot, finely chopped
- 1 clove of garlic minced to a paste
- 1 red chilli - deseeded and finely chopped
- 1 tbs oyster sauce
- 1 tsp fish sauce
- 2 tbs wine vinegar
- 1 tbs honey
- Soy sauce, adjust to taste
- Juice of 1 lime
- 4-5 kaffir lime leaves, crushed, stalks removed
- Lemon grass, crushed
- Fresh chopped coriander

METHOD

Mix all ingredients together and season to taste. Allow to infuse. Remove the lemon grass. Add chopped coriander just before serving.

Great with grilled red meats and salt-cured fish.

creole sauce

Good with pasta or gnocchi, etc

INGREDIENTS

- 120g onion, sliced
- 80g garlic, chopped
- 35g ginger, peeled and chopped
- 75g mixed dried herbs
- 35g tomato paste
- 75g sugar, honey or agave
- 350g tomato sauce, as p 47
- Chilli to taste, seeded and finely chopped
- Salt and pepper
- Olive oil

METHOD

Sauté the onions, ginger and garlic with some olive oil until it's soft and you get that lovely aroma (about 5-10 minutes).

Add mixed herbs and tomato paste - cook some more. Then add the tomato sauce and sugar. Bring to the boil, then simmer until soft. Then liquidise and if desired, pass through sieve.

Use as sauce with grilled meats or fish or pasta.

satay sauce

Delicious with skewered prawns or chicken

- Sesame, coconut or olive oil
- 1 large onion, finely chopped
- 4 cloves garlic, crushed
- 4 cm fresh ginger, finely chopped
- 1 tsp ground coriander
- 1 tsp ground cumin
- 2 red chillies + 1 green chilli (the small very hot ones, or adjust accordingly), seeded and finely chopped
- 30g brown sugar
- 3 tbs dark soy sauce
- 100ml chicken stock
- 1 glass of white wine
- 1 tbs lemon juice
- 200ml coconut milk
- 125g peanuts, finely chopped
- 1 bunch of fresh coriander

METHOD

Sauté the onion, ginger and garlic in the oil of your choice until soft, then lightly brown. Add the ground spices and chillies and mix well over low heat. Then add the sugar, soy, stock and wine. Allow the sugar to dissolve and the wine to reduce a little, then add the lemon juice and coconut milk. Bring to boil and reduce till you have a coating consistency.

If you are grilling satay sticks of meat or prawns or such, then baste them with the sauce as is and then just before serving add the peanuts and coriander, saving a little coriander to sprinkle over the cooked skewers. If using wooden skewers, soak them in water for 30 minutes before skewering your meat, prawns etc - this will stop the skewers from burning.

great tomato sauce

Great with all grilled meats and fish

INGREDIENTS

- Tomatoes - juice them or pass them through a sieve at the end
- Onions - finely chopped
- Garlic - crushed to a paste with rock salt
- White wine

METHOD

If you have a juicer (highly recommended for all kitchens!) then it is very quick and simple. Sauté the onions in olive oil and sprinkle with salt (it helps stop them from catching too quickly). Add the garlic when the onion starts to soften, then allow all to brown slightly. Add some white wine and bring to boil. Then add the tomatoes.

Cook until you have the desired consistency - if your tomatoes weren't overly sweet you can always add some brown sugar to make up for it. If you want the sauce completely smooth. Mix with a hand-held mixer - then pass through a sieve ('passez au chinois' sounds so much better!)

Add any fresh herbs, finely chopped according to the dish you are working with. Season with salt and pepper.

MAIN COURSE DISHES

Meat, poultry, fish and shellfish

prawns with passionfruit sauce

Decadence! The passionfruit acidity blends perfectly with the cognac and cream to enhance the prawns

INGREDIENTS

- **6 passionfruits - strain the fruit so you have no pips**
- **1 tsp ginger, finely chopped**
- **1 shallot, finely chopped**
- **100g butter**
- **4 tbs cognac**
- **125g cream**
- **Prawns - allow 5-6 per person depending on size**

METHOD

Prepare the passionfruit juice. Place a sieve over a measuring jug. Cut the passionfruits in half and scrape out the contents with a small spoon into a sieve. With the back of the spoon, extract as much juice as possible, leaving just the dark pips behind. Discard pips.

Prepare the prawns - remove head, shell and legs. You can butterfly down the back and remove the dark 'vein', if you want. Keep the shells and heads to roast and make a wonderful sauce. Sauté the ginger, shallots and garlic. Remove from pan and set aside. Then sauté the prawns in coconut oil - in a hot pan, until nicely coloured and cooked through. Remove and set aside with the ginger and garlic mix.

Deglaze the pan with the cognac. Add the cream, reduce, add the passionfruit juice, reduce, add the butter, taste and season - Add the prawns, ginger and garlic... yum!

salmon fillet saltimbocca
with citrus sauce

Almost literally jumps into the mouth!

INGREDIENTS

- Salmon fillet, with skin off. Do this with a sharp filleting knife or ask your fishmonger to do it for you.
- Parma ham

For sauce:

- Juice of 1 grapefruit
- 1 lemon
- 1 lime
- 1 orange
- 1 red chilli - deseeded and finely chopped
- Olive oil
- 1 tsp icing sugar
- Handful coriander - finely chopped
- 1 tsp soy sauce, or tamari if gluten free

METHOD

Cut the salmon into 4 cm wide pieces and wrap the salmon fillets round the middle with the Parma ham, overlapping underneath the salmon. Place on a baking sheet lined with baking paper.

Place in hot oven for 7 minutes, depending on the size of your fillets.

The Parma ham must have just got crisped on the top, yet the fillets should be just cooked through, with some dark pink in the middle.

For the sauce - juice the citrus fruits. Mix the icing sugar with the olive oil, making a paste, then add the rest of the ingredients, except the corainder. Reduce to desired consistency. Season. Add coriander.

Julienned courgettes, sautéed in some olive oil with ginger are a wonderful vegetable with this. Serve with a tower of courgettes.

Allow 130g-150g salmon per person.

thai-style prawns

Deliciously aromatic and lightly spiced

INGREDIENTS

- 20-24 prawns (5-6 per person), depending on size
- 1 tbs minced ginger
- 1 shallot, finely chopped
- 1 tbs coconut oil
- Handful each of basil and coriander leaves, torn
- 125ml coconut milk
- 1 glass white wine
- Kaffir lime leaves - crushed
- 1 lime - juice and zest
- Lemon grass - crushed

METHOD

Shell the prawns. Sauté the ginger and shallot together in the coconut oil. Remove from pan and set aside. Add prawns to same pan and cook on high heat till good colour, then lower heat - depending on size approximately 3 minutes. Remove prawns. Heat pan and de-glaze with wine - scraping all the bits. Add coconut milk and kaffir lime leaves, some fresh lime zest, lime juice and lemon grass, then add the ginger and shallot. Reduce to coating consistency.

To serve, either add the prawns to the sauce or serve separately, sprinkled with the basil and coriander leaves.

Serves 4.

seared sea bream fillets

Easy, healthy and full of flavour

- 1 sea bream fillet per person - ask your fishmonger to prepare them, skin on
- Egg white
- Seasoned flour
- Sesame seeds
- Butter and olive oil
- Lemon - quartered, pips out

METHOD

Prepare rice. Steam or cook the vegetables in some olive oil. If steamed, then refresh in cold water to maintain their colour. When ready to serve, heat rice and vegetables through in a little lightly-salted butter or olive oil. Add a handful of goji berries to the rice at the same time as the vegetables, so they have enough time to absorb/rehydrate. You do not want to soak the goji berries first – this makes them soggy.

Tomato sauce, see recipe p 47, heat through.

Mix one teaspoon of flour with one teaspoon of sesame seeds and season. Brush the skin with a little egg white, then dust fish fillet with seasoned sesame seeds. Heat oil and butter in a pan and cook the fish skin side down, with a good squeeze of fresh lemon juice. Leave the squeezed lemon in the pan. When pan is hot, place fillet with the sesame seed and skin side down and cook until the seeds are well browned, about 3-4 minutes depending on the thickness - you can see the flesh side just starting to cook. When it is cooked half way through, just flip over for one minute and serve.

Serve with black rice with finely chopped sautéed vegetables and tomato sauce (see pp 38 and 47).

fillet of cod with chorizo

Any firm white fillet will work with this

- **600g fish - filleted and cut into portion sizes**
- **Lemon zest**
- **Dill**

- **Butter or olive oil**
- **Chorizo, 10-12 cm piece**

Peel the chorizo skin off and cut into sticks about 4 cm long, and in a dry pan cook until very lightly browned on all sides – watch carefully, it takes less than a minute. Drain on absorbent paper. Keep warm. It should be crispy.

Wedge a baton down the centre of the fillet. Dust the fillets with some seasoned flour, lemon zest and dried dill, then cook in a shallow pan with a dash of oil and some butter, crisp on one side, then flip over and it should be cooked through, depending on the thickness of your fillets.

Serve with some puréed vegetables or some potatoes, boiled then crushed with olive oil, garlic mashed to a paste and seasoning. Serve the rest of the batons of chorizo on the side.

Serves 4.

turkey saltimbocca with sage butter

Saltimbocca means "jump in the mouth" - or in practice, wrapped in Parma ham.

- 6 turkey escalopes
- 6 slices of Parma ham
- 6-8 mushrooms, finely chopped
- 1 onion or shallot, finely diced
- 1 courgette, chopped into small dice

- 1 tbs chickpea flour
- Egg, broken into ramekin and mixed
- Butter
- Fresh sage leaves

METHOD

Get your butcher to cut six decent escalopes from the turkey breast and flatten them - you can do this with rolling pin, placing the escalope between sheets of baking paper.

To make the filling, sauté the finely chopped onion in some olive oil, add courgette, sauté till softened and lightly browned. Remove. Add mushrooms, sauté until all juice has evaporated and mushrooms are lightly golden. Add to courgette and onions - allow to cool. Add some egg and then chick pea flour to get the consistency of a stuffing. Season.

Place a slice of Parma ham on some baking paper, place the escalope on top at right angles - put a spoonful of filling in the middle and fold in the turkey breast, placing a whole sage leaf between turkey and ham, then wrap the ham.

Sear the turkey off in a pan, then cook in oven 180°C for 15 minutes. Deglaze the pan with some white wine, reduce, add some butter, chopped sage and season. When the turkey is removed from the oven, allow it to sit for 5 minutes. Cut the turkey on the diagonal and serve with sauce.

Sauté some whole sage leaves in salted butter and use as a crispy green garnish.

Alternative filling

- Cream cheese or boursin
- Sun-dried tomatoes, chopped
- Fresh sage leaves, chopped

Mix together and season. Then use as above.

Serves 6.

fillet of rabbit

Extremely lean white meat - tastes very like chicken

- 2 saddles of rabbit
- 1 carrot
- 1 onion
- Butter
- 250ml red wine
- Splash of balsamic vinegar
- 1 tsp Dijon mustard
- Lemon juice
- Olive oil
- Seasoning

METHOD

Bone the fillets by cutting lengthwise along the backbone, keeping the knife against the bone and then the whole fillet can be "rolled" out. Cut the flanks away and set aside, later these can be rubbed with olive oil, salt and pepper and cooked in hot oven for 15 minutes - a crispy contrast. Separate the kidneys.

Roughly cut the onions and carrot and brown in saucepan in some olive oil. Add the bones and brown them, then add the red wine. Reduce, then add some water to cover. Simmer for 20 minutes or so, then pass through a sieve, keeping just the liquid. Add the vinegar and mustard. Reduce in small saucepan. Season.

Trim the kidneys, discarding any fat and removing the membrane. Cut into quarters. Rub the fillets with olive oil and salt and pepper. Sear the fillets, then transfer to oven at 160°C for 4 minutes. Let sit, then slice at an angle to serve. Drizzle with lemon and oil mix. Season.

While the fillets are 'sitting', cook the chopped kidneys in butter, season with salt and add to the sauce just before serving.

Serves 4.

lamb tagine

Tasty and extremely tender

- Leg of lamb or shoulder - boned and cut into chunks
- 1 tsp each of cayenne pepper, paprika, ground gingor, turmeric and cinnamon
- Zest of 1 lemon
- 2 onions, peeled and diced
- Garlic - 2 cloves
- 500g tomato juice
- 400g tin of chopped tomatoes
- 100g each dried apricot and prunes, stones out
- 1 tbs honey
- Saffron powder
- Veal stock
- Smoked almonds, chopped
- Fresh coriander

METHOD

Dust the meat with the spices and zest. Leave overnight in the fridge.

In a large ovenproof dish, cook the onions and garlic in a little olive oil, then add the meat, tomato juice, tinned tomatoes, saffron, honey and stock.

Place in a casserole dish and cook in oven on low heat 130°C for 2½ hours. Stir and add the dried apricots and prunes. Cook for a further 30 minutes. Stir, taste and season.

Sprinkle with the chopped smoked almonds and coriander to garnish.

Serve with aromatic couscous.

Serves 6-8.

fillet of pork in parma ham

Depending on the size of the fillet, you will generally need one for three people

INGREDIENTS

- Pork fillets
- 3 slices of Parma ham per fillet
- Fresh spinach leaves
- Grainy mustard
- Red wine jus (see p 102)

METHOD

Trim the fillets. Lightly steam the spinach leaves, for less than 1 minute - just to make them soft and pliable. Then lay out one piece of baking paper per fillet. On the baking paper, spread out the 3 slices of Parma ham lengthwise, overlapping so that they form a rectangle. Then cover this with the wilted spinach, spreading out each leaf so you have one thin layer of spinach. Rub the mustard round the trimmed pork fillet and place this across the spinach. Then wrap the fillet with the ham with the spinach in between, making the Parma ham overlap round the fillet. Use the baking paper to assist the rolling process. The dish can be prepared to this stage in advance and kept in the fridge.

Remove from fridge for 30 minutes before cooking. Heat the oven to 200°C.

You do not need to seal the meat first. You can pop it directly into the preheated oven on an oiled Tefal baking sheet, or a silicone mat.

Cook for 12-15 minutes depending on the size. You can feel the Parma ham will be crispy and the meat firm, but with some give. You want it to be pink in the middle when you serve it.

Remove from the oven and let sit at least 5 minutes before you cut and serve.

Serve with a red wine jus and puréed pumpkin or sweet potato - the colour is great - or any mixture of puréed vegetables.

chicken thighs with lemon & thyme

Versatile dinner dish - easy to prepare in advance

- 6 chicken thighs, bone in
- Chopped fresh parsley to garnish

For the marinade:

- Red wine vinegar
- Thyme
- Bay leaf
- Garlic - crushed to a paste
- White wine
- Tamarind paste - made from fresh tamarinds, if possible
- Preserved lemon - chopped
- Onions - diced and sautéed in olive oil
- Green olives - stoned
- Capers
- Prunes - stoned and chopped roughly
- Brown sugar

METHOD

Mix all the ingredients together and allow the chicken to marinate for 3 to 24 hours. Then place in oven dish, pour marinade over the chicken and sprinkle with brown sugar. Roast at 180°C for 50 minutes. It is good to have the chicken skin crispy, so you might need to switch to the grill for an extra 10 minutes at the end. Remove any excess fat and serve garnished with chopped parsley.

Serve with brown rice and lentils, cooked in some stock. Sauté some onions and when starting to brown add some ground nutmeg, ground cinnamon, toasted pistachios, chopped parsley, chopped coriander, salt and pepper. Mix in the rice and lentils. Adjust seasoning, with a squeeze of lemon juice.

duck breast cooked at low temperature

Deliciously tender and beautifully pink

INGREDIENTS

- **Duck breast (2 people per breast)**
- **Bay leaf, salt and pepper**
- **Ziploc bag and straw or vacuum packer**

METHOD

Take the breast and score the fat in a diagonal pattern - make sure you do not cut through to the meat. Season with salt and pepper and a bay leaf. Place in bag - remove air and seal.

Place in a bain marie in oven at 70°C for 75 minutes. Remove from oven, take out the duck breast and drain it on absorbent paper. Set aside until 10 minutes before you want to serve.

Then salt the fat and place duck breast skin side down in pan over low heat - allow the fat to sizzle away, draining off as necessary so it does not spit. Up the heat to crisp the skin - press down with back of fork if necessary. When all fat removed, turn duck over and remove from pan.

Keep the dish warm while you prepare the plates. Then slice, plate and serve.

Excellent with puréed celeriac and Thai sauce drizzled round.

beef carpaccio

Carpaccio means 'thinly sliced'

- Fillet of beef, approx 125g per person
- Olive oil
- Juice of 1 lemon
- Capers or caper berries
- Shavings of Parmesan
- Roquette salad leaves
- Generous freshly ground black pepper

METHOD

Place your fillet in the freezer until it is very firm but not frozen solid - unless you are lucky enough to have a slicing machine, and then you can do it straight from the freezer. Chilling the meat just makes it easier to slice very thinly. Using a very sharp knife, slice as thinly as you can.

On the plates that you are going to serve on, drizzle a little olive oil - then start placing the slices in a circular pattern, overlapping as you go round until the whole plate is covered. At this point you can cover with cling film and place in the refrigerator.

When ready to serve, drizzle a little more olive oil, mixed with the lemon juice, over the meat. Dot the dish with some capers or caper berries, sprinkle the shavings of parmesan. Then put a bunch of freshly-dressed roquette or other salad leaves in the middle and give it a good grind of black pepper.

tortellini with a variety of fillings

No end of possibilities with fillings

- **1 lot of pasta dough (see p 102), divided into two**

For tortellini - make filling - here are a few ideas:

Mushroom filling

Sauté the finely chopped shallot in a little olive oil, then add chopped mushrooms, cèpes if possible. When nicely browned and any liquid cooked off, remove from heat and allow to cool. Then add ricotta and herbs. Use as below, then serve with truffle oil, shavings of fresh truffle if possible, Parmesan and black pepper.

Basil, mozzarella and tomato filling

Mozzarella 1 packet (approximately 175g), bunch of basil chopped and 5-6 chopped sun-dried tomatoes - mix ingredients with fork. Season. Use as below. Serve just with freshly chopped fresh basil, Parmesan and olive oil.

Lobster filling

Cooked lobster meat, chopped. Sauté some chopped shallot in olive oil and season with paprika, thyme and seasoning. Use as below, then serve with rich lobster sauce made from the shells and heads of the lobster meat - roast the shells first, then make a stock and reduce, add tomato purée. Serve with fresh snipped chives over the top and finally, a good burst of freshly ground black pepper.

METHOD (HAVING MADE YOUR FILLING)

Have a ramekin containing a raw egg mixed with dash of milk ready at the side. Dust your worktop generously with flour so the dough cannot stick. Roll out the dough very thin and then cut into circles using cookie cutters or a glass - approximately 5 cm in diameter. Place a small amount of filling in the centre of each circle. Then dip your finger in the egg mix and run it round the edge of the circles. Then with clean fingers pick up each circle and fold over, squeezing out any air, and pinch the edges firmly together. Then, wrapping it round your thumb or forefinger, whichever feels easiest, bring the edges of the half-moon circle together and pinch together and at the same time, the curved part will curl over a little, giving you the classic form of tortellini. Twist slightly. Place on floured baking paper and leave until the pasta has dried. Continue until all filling is used. At this point they can be frozen on baking paper. When frozen you can store them in an airtight container.

When ready to eat, fill a large saucepan with salted water and bring to the boil. Drop in the prepared pasta shapes and when they rise to the surface, they are ready to be removed with a slotted spoon. Keep warm until all the pasta is cooked. Then serve with the sauce, Parmesan, olive oil etc as chosen or as suggested above and a good turn of freshly-ground black pepper.

asparagus risotto

Try adding a seared scallop or two

- 250g asparagus spears
- Olive oil
- Butter
- 360g arborio rice
- Chicken stock, 800ml, warm
- 1 onion, chopped finely
- Glass of white wine
- 1 tbs Mascarpone
- 60g grated Parmesan

METHOD

Cut or break off the woody ends of the asparagus and discard, then cut the spears into approximately 8 cm long pieces. The remaining bits, slice thinly and evenly. Steam the asparagus tips, then refresh in iced water for 1 minute. Then drain.

Sauté the onion together with some olive oil and a knob of butter. When soft, add the asparagus bits and sauté for a few minutes. Reduce heat, then add the rice, until it is well coated with the oil and butter. Then add the wine. Allow to reduce, After a couple of minutes start adding the warm stock little by little, stirring all the time - this will take about 17 minutes. You might not incorporate all the stock. The rice should be slightly firm to the bite. The dish should be 'loose'. Add more stock if required.

Then add the Parmesan to the rice and stir. Add the Mascarpone and stir. Season and taste - adjust accordingly.

Sauté the asparagus tips in olive oil to heat through, then season.

Serve in bowls, with the asparagus tips arranged on top. Drizzle with olive oil and black pepper.

gnocchi with a variety of sauces

Can be used as an accompaniment for a meat dish or stand-alone dish – great for lunch with a mixed leaf salad

- 145-180g flour
- 500g potatoes
- 30g grated Parmesan
- 1 egg

- Nutmeg
- Salt and pepper
- Spinach - cooked, really well squeezed out and puréed (optional)

METHOD

Boil the potatoes in their skins, starting with cold water - you want to keep the starch in. The potatoes must be well cooked, but not overcooked. Measure the flour out. Skin the potatoes when they are still hot. Then either put them through a ricer or a large sieve, or grate them finely onto a floured work surface to cool, just enough so that when you add the egg it won't cook. Use the flour that you have measured. You can do this on the work surface or gently in a food processor – unlike pasta, gnocchi wants as little handling as possible. So if you do use a food processor, it must be extremely gentle pulses or you'll end up with rubbery gnocchi!

If on work surface, sprinkle more flour over the potatoes and form a well. Mix the egg, salt, nutmeg and pepper together. Pour over the potatoes and then sprinkle some more of the flour. Mix lightly with your fingers to form a dough. If the mixture is too tacky, add more flour. If using spinach, you'll need the larger quantity of flour.

Divide into eight parts. Roll out into long sausages, on a floured worktop with floured hands. Cut into 2 cm pieces. Press these segments onto the tine of a fork with your thumb, then roll over and lift off. This gives the classic indentation of gnocchi.

Place on floured baking paper on a tray, not touching, until all are prepared. At this stage, you could freeze it for a later date. When frozen, you can transfer from the baking tray to a plastic bag.

Plunge the gnocchi into boiling salted water and wait until they rise to the top. Do this in small batches. Then lift them out with a slotted spoon and place in dish with a small layer of sauce at the bottom and keep them warm.

Serve with any number of sauces:

Sage 'beurre noisette' – heat the butter and sage leaves until the butter starts to colour and the sage leaves are crisp. Remove the sage leaves and drain on paper towel. Season the butter with salt and pepper and spoon over the gnocchi. Add shavings of fresh Parmesan and the crisp sage leaves.

Creamy Gorgonzola – mix some chicken stock and cream with a splash of white wine. Bring to the boil and reduce for a few minutes. Remove from heat and add the Gorgonzola, then mix together and spoon over the warm gnocchi.

For a tomato sauce, see p 47.

DESSERTS

fruit salad with
lavender-infused syrup

INGREDIENTS

- **500g fruit in season**
- **200ml water**
- **80g sugar**
- **Bunch of fresh basil or mint or 4 sprigs of lavender**

METHOD

Dissolve the sugar in the water by heating gently and stirring until all crystals have dissolved. Then pour into bowl with the herbs or the lavender and cover with clingfilm to infuse for 20 minutes.

Strain and allow to cool, then refrigerate.

Peel the fruit as necessary and chop it into small, even, dice-sized pieces. Place in bowls. Then pour over syrup and serve with a scoop of ice cream or fruit sorbet.

Serves 6.

caramel fondant & caramel

A sure winner

INGREDIENTS

- 110g caramel - keep a batch ready in the fridge, it stores well
- 60g butter
- 2 eggs
- 60g sugar
- 70g flour

METHOD

Place caramel in glass bowl. Heat in microwave for 15 seconds or until soft. Add the butter so it can melt and mix in. The mixture should only be lightly warm, so allow to cool if too hot. Add the eggs and mix. Add the sugar and flour and mix well. You can prepare to this stage in advance.

Butter some small ramekins or moulds, then dust with sugar. Make sure the surface is covered, as this allows the mixture to rise on cooking and not to stick for turning out. It also very delicately crisps the outside.

Spoon the mixture into moulds, nearly to the top. Heat oven to 220°C and cook for 8-10 minutes, depending on the size of your mould. Let sit for a minute until you turn out. Serve with ice cream and a drizzle of the caramel base (reheated in the micro). Be careful, it heats very quickly - 30 seconds is enough!

Serves 6-8.

CARAMEL SAUCE INGREDIENTS

- 200g caster sugar
- Lime juice - a few drops, must be passed through a sieve so you don't get any flesh
- 150g single cream
- 85g salted butter

METHOD

Heat the sugar with some drops of lime juice and keep stirring until all is coloured and liquid. You must achieve a caramel colour, but do not burn it. Then take off heat and add the cream and butter chopped into small dice-sized pieces - it will bubble ferociously. Stir well, return to heat and stir further until you have a smooth, glossy beautiful caramel.

When cool pour into a glass jar and store in fridge. Use as required.

fruit & frangipane tart with sable crust

Frangipane was named after an Italian perfumier working in Paris in the 17th century

INGREDIENTS

- Fruit - 6-10 depending on whether you are using apricots, nectarines, figs or apples
- 300g sable pastry (see p 103)
- 3 eggs
- 100g milk
- 75g sugar
- 80g ground almonds

- Almond essence
- 75g plain flour

For the glaze:
- Apricot jam - 3 tbs
- Lemon juice - 2 tbs
- Water (add if too thick)

METHOD

Roll out the pastry to fit your dish (28-30 cm) and cut to size. Prick the bottom of the pastry. Place in refrigerator. After 30 minutes, pre-heat oven to 180°C with metal oven tray in oven.

In a measuring jug, measure the milk, add the eggs, almond essence - mix well with fork. Add sugar, flour, ground almonds and mix to combine - do not overmix.

Place the tart tray or dish on the hot baking tray in the oven and bake the pastry case 'blind' for 10 minutes with baking paper and weights. Then remove the paper and weights and return to oven for a further 5-10 minutes.

Prepare the fruit - for nectarines or apricots halve them, take stone out and cut into thin wedges. Figs should be quartered. For apples, peel, quarter, core and then cut into thin wedges.

Pour the filing into the pastry case and line the fruit on top. Return to oven for 25-30 minutes or until firm to the touch.

Meanwhile make the glaze - jam, lemon juice and water, if necessary - heat and pass through a sieve, then brush over the tart edges and fruit.

Serves 8-10.

chocolate fudge cake dessert

Wickedly rich, yet gluten free

- 200g butter, cut into small pieces
- 300g dark chocolate 85% cocoa, broken into small squares
- 300g brown sugar and 4 tbs of water
- 5 eggs, separated
- Pinch of salt

For the topping:
- 150g chocolate and 100g cream

METHOD

Place butter and chocolate into a large heatproof mixing bowl. Put the sugar and water into a saucepan and gently heat through till it is syrupy and all sugar has dissolved. Pour sugar mix over chocolate and butter. Stir until all is melted and you have a lovely thick chocolatey mix.

When cool, add the egg yolks to the chocolate mixture. Beat each one in well. In a separate bowl, whisk the egg whites with a good pinch of salt to form soft peaks, then fold into the chocolate mix. Pour into a prepared 30 cm tin lined with greaseproof paper.

Pop into a preheated oven at 170°C for 1 hour.

Remove. Let sit 5 minutes and then lightly press any air pockets out of the top of the cake with your hands - allow to cool completely.

For the topping, break the chocolate into pieces. Heat the cream to just before boiling, pour over chocolate and stir until you have a lovely velvety chocolate mixture. When the cake is turned out onto the serving dish you can pour the chocolate over and smooth with a palette knife to ensure even coverage. Dip the palette knife into a mug of boiling water if it sticks.

To elegantly serve as a dessert, slice into slim pieces and decorate, adding a fresh fruit coulis or a caramel drizzle if you like. Add fresh berries, mint leaves or similar.

Serves 12-16, freezes well.

tarte Tatin with apples or pears

The classic French upside-down tart

INGREDIENTS

- 8-10 apples - golden delicious or similar, peeled, cored and halved
- Caster sugar to cover bottom of tart pan
- 200g sweet pastry

METHOD

Use a 28 cm metal tart dish. Roll out the pastry to fit the dish perfectly and place on a baking tray in the fridge. It will be thicker than you would roll for a regular tart. Cover the bottom of the dish with the sugar and place over low heat - watch carefully, as you want the sugar to caramelise but not burn. Then put the apple halves into the dish, positioning them around the edge with the cut sides angled upwards. Continue into the centre until the apples fill the dish.

When all is tightly packed, put in oven at 190°C for 20 minutes. Then remove from oven and place pastry over fruit, covering it and touching the edges of the dish. Pop back in the oven for a further 35 minutes.

Allow to cool for at least 15 minutes before turning out. To turn out, place a serving platter which is larger than the tart dish on top of the tart, upside down so that when you flip it over, the tart will be with its pastry on the serving platter and the fruit on top. Always use a folded tea towel or oven gloves so that you hold the tart tin firmly to the plate, and turn the dish away from you when you flip it over.

Serve with crème fraîche.

Serves 8-10.

crème brûlée

With a few variations - if you choose

- 550g double cream
- Vanilla pod
- 4 egg yolks
- 2 tbs of caster sugar
- Icing sugar for the brûlée

METHOD

Beat the sugar and eggs together in a measuring jug. In a medium-size heavy-bottomed saucepan, heat the cream with the vanilla pod and its seeds. Cut the pod down the middle lengthwise and scrape out with a knife. Do not boil. Remove vanilla pod. You can rinse, dry and use to make vanilla sugar. Pour the cream over the egg mix. Stir well, then return to the saucepan and heat until it thickens. Strain, then pour into the ramekins.

Place a thin layer of fruit at the bottom if you wish - peeled and seeded green grapes are wonderful.

Place the ramekins in a large ovenproof roasting dish and pour water round the ramekins so the water helps to cook the 'custards'. This is called a bain marie. Cook at 130°C for 35-40 minutes.

Remove. Allow to cool, then place in fridge for at least 6 hours. Just before serving, cover with icing sugar and blow torch to crisp the top.

Variations:

85g white or dark chocolate added to the hot strained liquid. These will require shorter time in the oven.

Fresh fruit, peeled, stoned or seeded such as nectarines, green grapes or apricots - enough to give a thin layer at the bottom of each ramekin.

Infuse jasmine or lavender into the cream, strain over egg mixture.

Serves 6-8, depending on size of your ramekins.

tartes fines
aux pommes

Sounds better in French but tastes exquisite in any language!

INGREDIENTS

- 300g puff pastry
- 3 apples or pears
- 100g butter

- 25g brown sugar
- Caster sugar
- Armagnac

METHOD

In a small heavy-bottomed saucepan, heat the butter until it starts to colour, then plunge saucepan into bowl of iced water to stop the cooking process - this is a 'beurre noisette' and can be stored in the fridge in a screw-top jar. Just re-heat in the microwave when required. It has a lovely nutty flavour.

Cut out circles of the puff pastry - approximately 12 cm diameter for individuals, or you can do a slightly larger one to be shared by two people. Place on metal baking sheets on baking paper.

Using a pastry brush, brush the pastry circles with the 'beurre noisette'. Thinly slice the cored and peeled apples and lay them in circular arrangement, overlapping, until all the pastry is covered. Butter again and dust with brown sugar and tiny knobs of butter.

Pre-heat oven to 190°C and cook tarts for 16-18 minutes. They should be lightly browned on top, with the pastry cooked through.

Heat some Armagnac in a ladle over a gas flame and when warmed, allow the liquid to catch and while flaming, pour it over the tart. Or heat in small saucepan and then set light to it with a lighter. If you want to do this at the table, shape the balls of ice cream beforehand and place in the freezer on a piece of baking paper. Then place in centre of tarts and flambé at the table.

Alternatively, serve with vanilla ice cream and a drizzle of caramel sauce.

Serves 6.

tiramisu

The classic version from Italy

INGREDIENTS

- 6 eggs, separated
- 6 tbs caster sugar
- 500g Mascarpone
- Vanilla essence, a few drops
- Boudoir biscuits x 60, or genoise sponge
- 125ml Amaretto
- 500ml strong coffee
- Cocoa for dusting

METHOD

Use a 20 cm x 30 cm rectangular dish. Beat the egg yolks with the caster sugar until they are ribbon like - thick and creamy and leaving a thick trail behind the whisk when you lift it out. Incorporate the Mascarpone to this mixture and add a few drops of vanilla essence. Mix well.

Whisk the egg whites with a pinch of salt until they form soft peaks. Fold into the egg yolk mixture.

Add the amaretto to the coffee in a dish large enough to lay the biscuits in down flat and submerge them in the liquid. Or cut out the sponge to the moulds or dish you want to use and drizzle with the liquid.

Dunk each biscuit in the liquid and on lifting out, turn each one end to end so it can absorb sufficient liquid. Place in a layer on the bottom of the serving dish, then layer half the Mascarpone mixture, another layer of sponge, then the rest of the mixture. Using a fine sieve, sprinkle cocoa in a thick layer over the entire surface. Place in fridge for at least 6 hours before serving. Best made day before.

To serve elegantly, cut into rectangular portions, use a spatula to lift out, then slide onto individual serving plates. Dust dish with cocoa or icing sugar depending on colour and maybe add some seasonal fruit garnish.

Serves 10-12.

tarte au citron

Truly delicious and extremely lemony

- 150g of lemon juice (approximately 4 lemons). Roll the lemons on your worktop to release the juices before cutting in half.
- 125g sugar
- 4 eggs
- 125g butter, chopped into small pieces
- Sweet pastry crust (see p 103) - baked blind

METHOD

Break the eggs into a large bowl (big enough to whisk) with the sugar and lemon juice. Whisk together, then place over a medium saucepan of water, so the bowl will not touch the hot water in the saucepan. Whisk constantly for 10-15 minutes, keeping the water just off the boil. When the mixture has thickened to a thick ribbon-like consistency, remove from the heat and whisk in the butter. Add butter in small pieces so it melts without needing further heating, but the mixture must not be so hot that it separates the butter. When all the butter has been incorporated, the mixture should be silky smooth, thick and delicious.

Spoon the mixture into the cooked tartlet tins or a single large tin. Allow to cool completely, then refrigerate, for at least 6 hours and preferably overnight.

Before serving, sprinkle with icing sugar and use a blow torch to 'brûlée' the top prior to serving.

Serve garnished with some fresh raspberries and a splash of raspberry coulis.

Serves 8-10.

nut bites

Excellent for that mid-afternoon 'pick me up'

INGREDIENTS

- 170g honey
- 45g butter
- 120g almonds, roughly chopped
- 120g pumpkin seeds
- 120g walnuts, roughly chopped
- A handful of goji berries
- 75g chocolate

METHOD

Heat honey and butter with a pinch of salt until caramel colour - lightly caramelised. Do not burn!

Fold in the chopped nuts and seeds.

Press into lined tin (20 cm x 25 cm). Press down with back of spoon (to stop it sticking, dip spoon into cup of boiling water). When tightly packed leave to cool. When cool, pop in fridge.

Melt chocolate. Turn the 'bite' tin out onto baking paper and cover the base with chocolate. Mark with the tines of a fork. When cool, return to fridge. When all is hard, cut into bite-size pieces and store in airtight container in the fridge.

Makes about 24 squares.

chocolate truffles

Squares or rounds rolled in cocoa or finely shredded coconut

- 200g chocolate, broken into small pieces
- 50g butter, chopped into small pieces
- 150g double cream
- 2 tbs brandy or champagne, which must be reduced first - 1 glass down to 2 tbs
- Salt

METHOD

Heat the cream to boiling, allow to reduce by 1/3, then, passing the cream through a sieve, pour over the chocolate and butter. Stir until glossy and smooth. Add the alcohol and a good pinch of salt.

For square truffles, pour the mixture into a rectangular 20 cm x 25 cm tin lined with baking paper and allow to set before cutting into squares.

For round truffles, let the mixture become firm and chill lightly, then spoon into balls and roll in your hands. Then roll in cocoa or shredded coconut.

Alternatives:

The mix can be used to stuff stoned prunes, which can then be left as is or dunked in melted chocolate and then rolled in cocoa - worth it!

Stone the prunes, then fill with the chocolate mix and close. Chill, then dip in melted chocolate. Allow to 'set' a bit, then roll in cocoa.

Makes about 30 balls or squares.

glossary & notes

I have tried to make the recipes simple to follow, with clear instructions. Always read the recipe the whole way through, before starting. Baking oven temperatures vary, humidity in kitchens varies and all these factors can affect the results, so when you are baking, please check 5-10 minutes before the end to see what is going on, whether too hot or too cool etc, and adjust accordingly. You might also need to turn your dish half way through cooking depending if your oven is hotter on one side than the other - some are! All oven temperatures are °C. Also, I use pink Himalayan salt throughout - the purest salt available, with great minerals.

BUTTER AND OIL

Butter will burn if heated too high on its own. Either use clarified butter or add a splash of olive oil to your cooking pan. To clarify butter - pop 250g of unsalted butter, chopped into chunks, into a saucepan and heat until all melted, then skim off the foamy frothy bits and let the milk solids fall to the bottom. Then pour through a muslin cloth, lining a sieve, leaving you with pure golden liquid butter. Store in airtight jar in fridge. Use as required.

COATING CONSISTENCY

Refers to when the liquid starts to cling to the back of a spoon.

DE-GLAZE

Refers to when you are adding a liquid to a hot pan - it could be stock, wine or other liquid. The aim with this is to get all the flavours that have come out in the earlier cooking process and gather them together to incorporate for the sauce.

BALSAMIC REDUCTION

Literally what it says - you reduce a quantity of balsamic vinegar at least by half to achieve a thicker, more intense liquid. I take a whole bottle and reduce it down to a quarter of the original amount. It is then very syrupy and can be used decoratively or as an addition.

DRIED BLACK OLIVES

Remove the stones from black olives - good quality full flavoured ones - and chop quite finely. Then place on baking paper on tray and bake at 60°C till they are well dried and crispy. Store in airtight jar and add to salads when you need a kick of salty flavour.

TAPENADE

100g black olives, stoned
1 big tbs capers
2 anchovies, well rinsed
1/2 garlic clove
Parsley or thyme - fresh 2 tbs
Olive oil approx 3-4 tbs
Juice of 1 lemon
Black pepper

Mix all ingredients together to a paste, as coarse or smooth as you like. Adjust the amount of olive oil at the end. Taste, then season.

SEGMENT A CITRUS FRUIT

Cut the top and bottom off. Then with a serrated knife, cut off all the skin and pith. If you want to use the zest, then cut that off first very thinly and then remove the pith, leaving yourself with the whole peeled fruit, flesh, pips and membrane only. Do this over a bowl. Then cut either side of the membrane and a perfect segment will drop into your bowl below. Remove pips where necessary. When all segments have been cut out, squeeze what you have left to extract all the juice.

PEELING AND SEEDING A TOMATO

Have ready a saucepan of boiling water, a slotted spoon and a bowl of iced water. Cut a tiny cross in the base of the tomato. Plunge the tomato into the boiling water and remove the moment you see the little cut start to pare back – 40 to 55 seconds, depending on the ripeness of the tomato. Remove with slotted spoon and put into iced water. Remove when cold, drain and the skin will peel off easily – generally into 4 sections which can be fried and used as edible garnish. Then quarter and cut the seeds and thicker part of the tomato out – you can use this to pop into salads – juicy seeds and pretty too. Or just remove the seeds and juice. You can use the juice to add to sauces. Don't waste! Use tomato flesh as required.

OVEN-DRIED TOMATOES

Using the tomato flesh quarters, as on p 101, you can lay them all out on a baking tray lined with baking paper, skin side down and sprinkle with herbes de Provence, salt and pepper and drizzle a little olive oil and pop them in the oven to dry at low temperature, 80°C for 2-3 hours.

BAIN MARIE

A water bath, used for cooking custard type dishes where a dish or ramekin is placed in a roasting pan, then water filled to 3/4 the way up the dish or ramekin. You can put a tea towel at the bottom to stop them sliding, but I just pop the ramekins in the roasting dish, pop in oven then fill up with water from a jug. At the end of the cooking time, I just lift out the ramekins with a tea towel and ensure I take the ones from the front first, not dripping any water over the remaining ones!

RED WINE JUS

1 carrot	1 shallot
White part of leek, optional	1 clove garlic, optional
Bay leaf	Thyme, rosemary etc
Red wine	Chicken stock

In some olive oil, sauté the carrot, shallot, leek and garlic, if using. When nicely browned, deglaze the pan with the red wine and allow to reduce. Add the stock and cook for a further 20 minutes or more if you have time. Strain and reduce to desired consistency. Season to taste.

A teaspoon of tomato purée or a splash of balsamic reduction can always be added.

PASTA DOUGH

INGREDIENTS

220g flour - type 55 is best, but any white flour is fine.

2 eggs

Pinch of salt

If used for shaped pasta, add 1 tsp of milk per egg.

If needing more, per extra two servings
add 110g flour/1 egg.

METHOD

Sift the flour out onto your work surface, create a hole in the middle and crack the eggs into that. Add a good pinch of salt. Mix the egg with the milk (if making shaped pasta) and with a fork start to slowly bring in the flour until it forms a ball, then start kneading. If dough is crumbly, add a teaspoonful of olive oil. If it sticks to your hands, add more flour to the work surface. Kneading brings out the gluten in the flour - knead for 10-15 minutes until the pasta is silky, smooth and elastic and bounces back to the touch.

For different colours and flavours, add puréed cooked and well-drained spinach, puréed cooked beetroot, tomato purée, squid ink etc. If using a vegetable purée, reduce the number of eggs.

OR make it in a food processor - put the flour in first and whizz with the salt - it saves sifting. Then add eggs and if using a flavouring/colour (puréed spinach, puréed beetroot, squid ink etc), add it now. Add 1 tsp milk at this point if using pasta for tortellini or ravioli. Pulse until it is just past the breadcrumb stage and turn out onto a floured surface. Then you need to knead for 10 minutes or until it is elastic and smooth and bounces back to the touch.

Wrap in cling film and leave to rest in fridge for 30 minutes. Divide into two to work with, either using a pasta machine or just a rolling pin is fine.

SWEET PASTRY FOR TARTS (SABLE CRUST)

INGREDIENTS

200g plain flour	Salt
85g icing sugar	Vanilla powder
100g butter	1 egg
15g ground almonds, optional	

METHOD

Sieve the dry ingredients into a large mixing bowl and mix together with fork. Chop butter through with knife until it forms breadcrumbs, using your fingers when necessary. Create a hole in the centre. Add mixed egg and incorporate with a fork. Make circular movements, 'bringing in' the flour mixture until you can use your hands to form a ball. Wrap in cling film and place in fridge for one hour before rolling out. Use as required.

Alternatively, if you are very gentle, you can use a food processor. Place the dry ingredients into the bowl of the food processor and pulse to mix - saves sifting. Then add the butter and pulse until it resembles fine breadcrumbs. Then add the egg and pulse gently until it just starts to stick together. You might have to add a tablespoon of cold water to make it form a ball. Then, using your hands, turn it out gently onto a floured work surface and form a ball. Wrap in cling film and place in fridge for one hour before rolling out. Use as required.

This quantity is sufficient for 6-8 individual tartlets or one large, 30 cm. Whatever is left over you can make into little sable biscuits and when cool, half dip in melted chocolate.

For the tarte au citron (26 cm tart tin or individual ones):

125g plain flour	75g butter
50g icing sugar	Salt
1 tsp sweet vanilla powder	15g ground almonds
1 egg	Method as above

TO STOP PASTRY SHRINKING

Minimum handling - do not try to play with it like pasta dough! Refrigerate before you roll out to your tart tins. Then return the tart tins lined with the pastry to the fridge for at least 30 minutes more. It's the moisture and the gluten in the pastry that causes the shrinkage so try not to add the extra water to mix and try not to overwork the pastry.

TO BAKE BLIND

Remove your lined tin from the fridge. Ensure you have pricked the base of the tart and line with baking paper, then fill with baking beans, lentils or other dried pulses. Ensure the beans are pushed to the edge to stop the edges 'falling in'.

Place in pre-heated oven, 170°C on metal oven tray. Cook for 10 minutes, then remove the baking paper containing the baking beans and return the tart to the oven and cook until it is an even golden brown.

WEIGHTS & MEASUREMENTS

In the recipes, all weights and measures are metric and tbs = tablespoon, and tsp = teaspoon. It's always easiest to weigh in grams using a little scale, but for those who prefer cup measurements or other, then here is an approximate conversion chart:

GRAMS/CUPS/US OZ

30g	= 1 oz
60g	= 2 oz
100g	= 3.5 oz
120g	= 4 oz
150g	= 5 oz
180g	= 6 oz
240g	= 8 oz
150g flour	= 1 cup/5 oz

240g caster sugar	= 1 cup/8 oz
180g brown sugar	= 1 cup/6 oz
240g butter	= 1 cup/8 oz
360g honey	= 1 cup/12 oz

OVEN TEMPERATURES

°C	°F	Gas Mark
230	450	8 very Hot
200	400	6 hot
180	350	4 moderate
150	300	2 slow
120	250	1 very slow

BASIC SUPPLIES

Olive oil	Balsamic vinegar
Other vinegars	Black pepper
Paprika	White pepper
Cayenne	Saffron
Nutmeg	Cardamom
Cinnamon	Ground ginger
Star anise	Tomato paste
Cumin, whole and ground	Soy sauce or tamari
Grapeseed oil	Celery salt
Turmeric	Different flours
Honey	Salt (I use Himalayan pink salt
Sugar	for all seasoning and regular
	salt for boiling, blanching etc)

Coriander seeds	Baking paper
Sesame seeds	Aluminum foil
Pumpkin seeds	Clingfilm
Mustard seeds	Paper towel
Caraway seeds	
Sunflower seeds	

ESSENTIAL UTENSILS

Good sharp knives

Vegetable peeler

Pestle and mortar

Palette knife

Tongs

Sieves of varying grades

Melon baller

Graters, different sizes

Measuring jugs

Tefal/silicon sheets

Baking trays

Tins, assorted sizes and shapes

Electric hand beater

Hand-held mixer

Mandoline

Rolling pin

Spatulas

index

CANAPES, STARTERS, VEGETABLES, SALADS AND MAINS

DESSERTS

JANE WHALLEY PROST

Flavours from the Flying Gourmet

Flavours from the Flying Gourmet 978-1-86151-259-8

First published in Great Britain in 2014 by Mereo Books, an imprint of Memoirs Publishing

The address for Memoirs Publishing Group Limited can be found at www.memoirspublishing.com

The Memoirs Publishing Group Ltd Reg. No. 7834348

The Memoirs Publishing Group supports both The Forest Stewardship Council® (FSC®) and the PEFC® leading international forest-certification organisations. Our books carrying both the FSC label and the PEFC® and are printed on FSC®-certified paper. FSC® is the only forest-certification scheme supported by the leading environmental organisations including Greenpeace. Our paper procurement policy can be found at www.memoirspublishing.com/environment

Typeset in 9/15pt Helvetica Thin by Wiltshire Associates Publisher Services Ltd.
Printed and bound in Great Britain by Printondemand-Worldwide, Peterborough PE2 6XD

Mereo Books
1A The Wool Market Dyer Street Cirencester, Gloucestershire GL7 2PR
An imprint of Memoirs Publishing www.mereobooks.com